THIS WALKER BOOK BELONGS TO:

_____

_____

_____

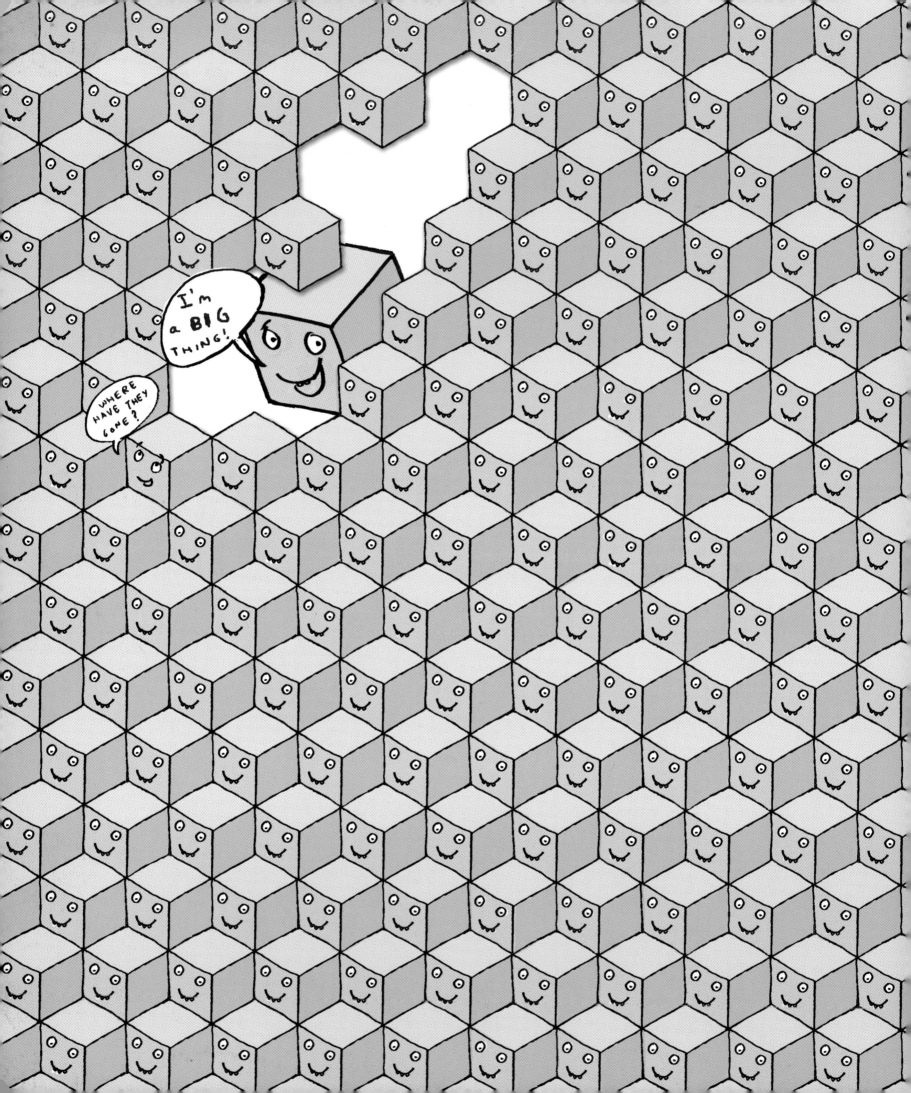

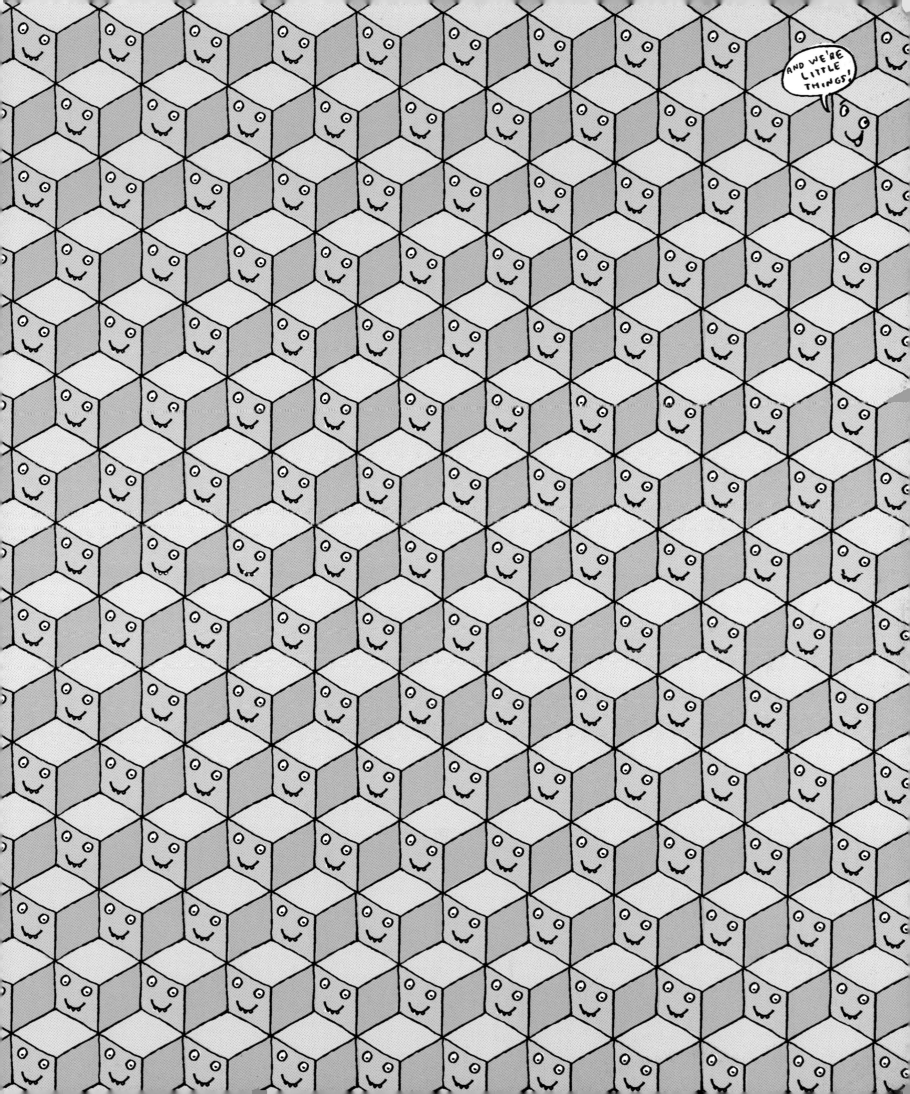

For Martin J. and the whale-sized teleosts   N. D.

For little tiny Erica Lavender   N. L.

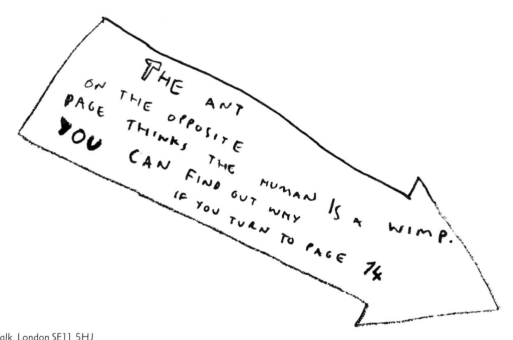

THE ANT ON THE OPPOSITE PAGE THINKS THE HUMAN IS A WIMP. YOU CAN FIND OUT WHY IF YOU TURN TO PAGE 14

First published 2009 by Walker Books Ltd, 87 Vauxhall Walk, London SE11 5HJ

This edition published 2014

10 9 8 7 6 5 4 3 2 1

Text © 2009 Nicola Davies   Illustrations © 2009 Neal Layton

The right of Nicola Davies and Neal Layton to be identified as author and illustrator respectively of this work has been asserted by them in accordance with the Copyright, Designs and Patents Act 1988

This book has been typeset in AT Arta

Printed in China

British Library Cataloguing in Publication Data: a catalogue record for this book is available from the British Library

ISBN 978-1-4063-5747-9

www.walker.co.uk

Just the Right Size

Why Big Animals are Big and Little Animals are Little

by **Nicola Davies**

illustrated by **Neal Layton**

WIMP!

WALKER BOOKS
AND SUBSIDIARIES
LONDON · BOSTON · SYDNEY · AUCKLAND

CREATURE SUPER HEROES

In comics and films, superheroes zoom across the sky,

run up walls, lift things as big as buses and

use their super powers to fight giant monsters!

It's all very exciting but it's a complete load of nonsense. Real humans can't fly, hang from the ceiling or even lift things much bigger than themselves ... and real giant animals couldn't exist — they wouldn't be able to walk or breathe.

You see there are very strict rules that control what bodies can and can't do: they keep creatures from getting too big and mean the *real* superheroes are usually small — a lot smaller than humans...

MEET SOME SMALL SUPERHEROES AND REAL GIANTS

Teeny **hummingbirds** and titchy **wasps** are the nimblest fliers on Earth.

Geckos no bigger than your hand can walk up walls or on ceilings.

Leafcutter ants are only 6 mm long and weigh less than 1 g, but can lift many times their own weight.

Rhinoceros beetles can carry 850 times their own weight.

The world's largest ape, the male **gorilla** is teeny compared to King Kong. At 1.68 m, he's probably just about as tall as your dad!

The biggest spider on Earth, the **Lasiodora spider,** is just 19 cm long — about the size of a dinner plate.

RULES AGAINST SUPER POWERS

So what *are* these rules that stop us from having super powers?

They aren't rules made by humans. You can disobey human rules like "no ice cream before you eat your broccoli" or "no parking here". Instead they are rules that are part of the way our universe is put together. You can't get around things like "light travels in straight lines" or "things on Earth fall downwards when you drop them". The rules that mean giant spiders only happen in cartoons and Superman isn't real (sorry) are rules of geometry – that's the kind of maths that's about size and shape.

The best way to explain these rules is to take a close look at the difference between little things and big things...

WOOF!

A LITTLE THING

Here is Little Thing – it could be anything, a car, a log, a bar of soap, but it just happens to be a creature (even if it looks a bit like a cube).

Let's take a few measurements of Little Thing...

how long it is (its length)

how big its outside is (its surface area)

DON'T FORGET THE SIDES YOU CAN'T SEE

how big a slice through its middle is (its cross section)

how much room it takes up (its volume)

and its weight

I THINK SO...

OK so far?

Now let's meet Big Thing. Big Thing is TWICE the size of Little Thing (that's to say Big Thing is twice as long, twice as wide and twice as tall).

Let's see how many Little Things it would take to make one Big Thing (remember Big Thing is twice as long as Little Thing)…

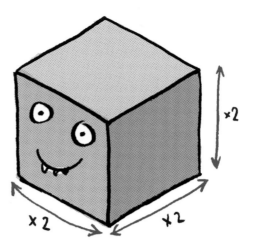

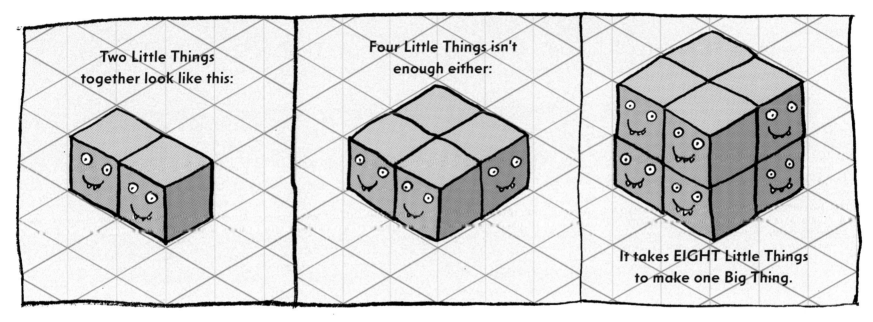

Two Little Things together look like this:

Four Little Things isn't enough either:

It takes EIGHT Little Things to make one Big Thing.

Now you can see Big Thing's surface area and cross section are four times bigger. But Big Thing's volume and weight are eight times bigger.

This rule, let's call it the Big Thing, Little Thing Rule, or BTLT for short, works on animals and plants and people and anything:

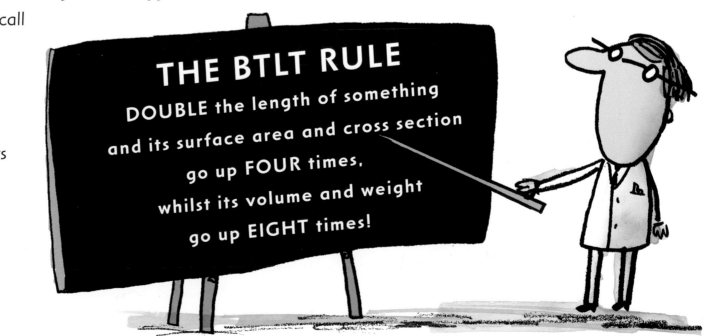

THE BTLT RULE
DOUBLE the length of something and its surface area and cross section go up FOUR times, whilst its volume and weight go up EIGHT times!

THE BTLT RULE – ALIVE!

The BTLT rule isn't just about numbers though. It has a big effect on how living bodies work. Some important features of bodies – like how much food and air they need – depend on volume and weight, and others – like the strength of muscles – depend on cross section or surface area.

It's easy to see that Big Thing is going to need as much food to eat and air to breathe as EIGHT Little Things. But if we take a slice through Big Thing we can see that its muscles are four times thicker than Little Thing's muscles … making it only four times stronger.

The BTLT rule makes some things quite impossible for bodies to do or be! It stops monsters such as car-sized spiders from existing in the real world, and it also means that humans can't lift buses and could never flap their arms and fly…

↰ 4 TIMES thicker than this →

HERE TODAY, SEE THE AMAZING FLYING BIRDMAN!!

OOPS...

DON'T FORGET THE BTLT RULE!!

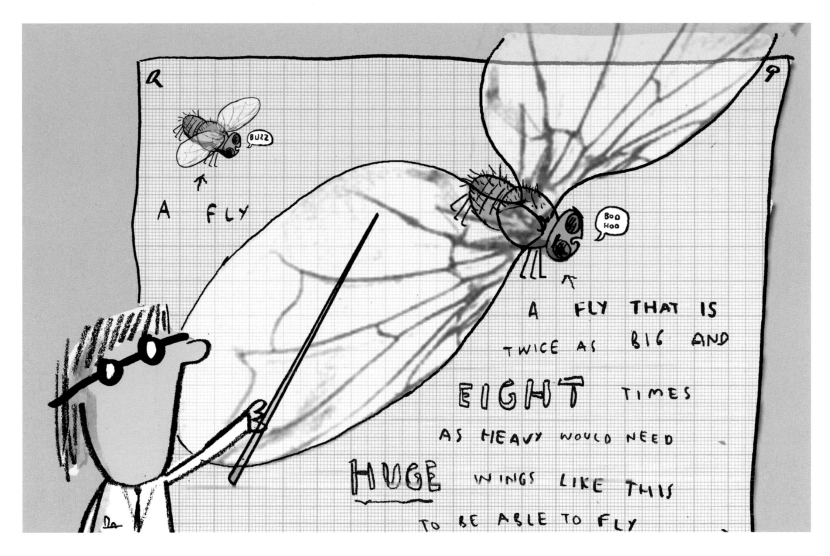

WHY HUMANS CAN'T TAKE OFF

For the very teeniest fliers, such as insects as small as one of these letters, take-off is easy. A puff of wind on their wings is enough to get them airborne. But because of the BTLT rule, flying gets harder the bigger you get.

If you could take an insect and make it twice as big – its outside (or surface area) will get four times bigger, which means its wings will also get four times bigger. Its muscles, too, will be four times thicker and so four times as strong (muscle strength depends on cross section – remember?) which would be fine if the insect was just four times heavier but, because of the BTLT rule, it weighs

EIGHT times more. So it's not going to be able to take off unless its wings and its muscles are much much bigger...

This is why heavier insects, like dragonflies, need very big wings to get them off the ground and birds need huge chest muscles and large, feather-covered wings.

But wings and muscles can't keep up with heavier and heavier bodies. That's why really big birds like ostriches and emus gave up flying and walk instead. And why the only way humans can fly is with the help of engines.

11

DANCING ON WATER

Look at the surface of a pond on a summer's day and you'll see insects called pond skaters perform the amazing feat of walking on water. So how come they can do it and we can't?

Water has a kind of thin skin where all the tiny particles that make the water line up. It's called the "surface tension" and it's what the pond skaters walk on. They spread their weight using long, skinny feet, like skates, so that they don't press too hard and push through the surface tension.

But if pond skaters were twice as long, the weight those feet would

have to hold up would be eight times bigger (remember the BTLT rule?), and their feet would need to be eight times longer. Rather too long to move, in fact…

And that's why you don't see animals bigger than pond skaters – such as humans – dancing on water: they would need ridiculously large feet!

EVEN THIS RIDICULOUSLY LONG FOOT WOULD NOT BE LONG ENOUGH

CLOSE-UP OF THE POND SKATER'S FOOT NOT BREAKING THE SKIN OF THE WATER

WALKING ON THE CEILING

It's a similar story with walking on the ceiling. Spiderman does it, but in real life the biggest ceiling-walkers are little lizards called geckos. They can even run up panes of glass, and hunt insects on the ceiling.

The secret's in their toes, which are shaped like flattened spoons. Under a microscope you can see that gecko toes are covered with thousands of tiny hairs. These hairs can fit tight onto the smoothest wall or pane of glass; so tightly that the microscopic forces that hold the tiny particles of the wall or window together, hold on to the hairs, sticking them fast. Adding up the stickiness acting on so many hairs gives enough sticking power to keep the gecko on the ceiling.

So why can't we have spoon-shaped "hairy toes" and run up walls like a gecko? The answer (of course!) lies in the BTLT rule. We weigh thousands of times more than a tiny gecko and we'd need toes tens of thousands of times bigger than a gecko's to hold us on the ceiling — much too big for running about without tripping!

13

WHY WE CAN'T LIFT BUSES

An ordinary ant can lift between ten and fifty times its own weight and a Rhinoceros beetle can carry 850 times its own weight on its back. Yet the best human weightlifters can only lift about four or five times their own bodyweight. How can little insects be stronger than big butch humans? It's the BTLT rule at work again.

Below is Little Thing. Let's say Little Thing can lift something as heavy as itself.

Also below is Big Thing. Because muscle strength depends on cross section, Big Thing is FOUR times stronger than Little Thing. So Big Thing can lift four times as much as Little Thing.

But because Big Thing *weighs* the same as EIGHT Little Things, Big Thing can't lift something as heavy as itself. It can only lift something *half* as heavy as itself.

That's how ants can be stronger than humans!

GETTING RID OF MONSTERS

I'm sorry if you are disappointed to hear that you will never be able to fly, sprint up windows, dance on ponds or be stronger than an ant. But as you can't be a superhero, the BTLT rule will do your monster-busting for you. Let me show you how. Let's start with a Terrible Tale of Giants...

Once upon a time there was a giant. Just like a normal human, only ten times bigger all over. Ten times taller and wider and deeper. Making him 1,000 times heavier. The giant took his first giant step, and with a giant crashing sound, both his legs snapped. The end.

(And exactly the same thing happened to the giant's best friend, the monster spider!)

Remember, strength doesn't keep up with weight, because strength depends on the size of the cross section. In this case, the cross section – or slice – through the giant's leg is a hundred times bigger than a normal human's, so only a hundred times stronger – much too weak to take the giant's huge weight, a thousand times greater than a normal human's!

A real twenty-metre-tall giant would need legs that weren't just bigger, but were so thick they would probably be too heavy to lift.

BIG, BIGGER, BIGGEST?

Legs can't go on getting stockier to hold up bigger and bigger animals, because stocky legs are heavy to move. Scientists think that this is what put an upper limit on the size of dinosaurs. The biggest dinosaur was 35 m long and weighed 100 tonnes. Any heavier and it would have needed legs too stocky to move.

So it's not surprising the heaviest animal that has ever lived doesn't need legs at all. The blue whale is 30 m long and weighs up to 190 tonnes – but as its weight is supported by sea water, why can't it be twice as big?

A double-sized, 60 m blue whale would have eight times the body volume of a 30 m whale: its gut would need to digest eight times more food, its lungs would need to breathe eight times more air and its kidneys get rid of eight times more wee than a 30 m whale. But internal organs get bigger with the area of a whale's cross section, so they'd only be four times larger than in a 30 m whale. A double-sized blue whale of 60 m would need guts, lungs and kidneys so big, that they wouldn't fit in its tummy.

Which probably explains why the biggest blue whale ever found was just 33.5 m long.

RULES ON THE INSIDE

As you can see from the story of the blue whale, the BTLT rule works on the insides of bodies as well as the outsides. It's been doing that since the start of life on Earth and it's had a big effect on how living things evolved, from simple to complicated.

Life on Earth first started (about 4,000 million years ago) with little creatures so small it would take more than fifty, laid end to end, to cross a full stop. They were really, reeeeeally simple – just one cell big with no mouth, guts or lungs. They didn't even have to breathe: they just floated around in water and the oxygen they needed could drift in, through their skin. That's because they had quite a big surface area, and a small volume. In other words, a lot of skin for not much body.

If such a creature were to double in size, it would have four times more surface area but eight times more volume. That means it would need eight times as much oxygen, but have only four times as much skin to get it through. If it went on getting bigger, pretty soon it would have too much body and not enough skin to get its oxygen through.

This is why simple, single-celled creatures can't get very big. To get big, living things had to get complicated…

AN ARTIST'S impression of Planet Earth 4,000,000,000 years ago...

A TINY SIMPLE CREATURE

A BIGGER SIMPLE CREATURE

A MUCH BIGGER SIMPLER CREATURE...

Aghh! CAN'T BREATHE...

FOLDS AND WRINKLES

One way for simple creatures to get more skin for getting oxygen through is to make their outer skin foldy to increase its surface area. That's exactly what a single-celled creature called Epulos does. It lives in the guts of fish and has a wrinkly, folded, pocketed skin. This allows it to be fifty times bigger than most other single-celled creatures.

But fifty times bigger is still only the size of a full stop and having the whole of your outside covered in crinkly skin gets in the way of having useful things like legs and heads. So bigger animals,

made of many many millions of single cells (each human is made of around 100,000 billion cells), have found that it's better to have all your foldy skin for getting oxygen in one place.

That's what gills are, many folds of thin skin that oxygen can pass through into the body, packed up into a small space. Most water-living animals have gills, but the best are fish gills. They have a BIG surface area, blood, blood vessels and a heart to pump oxygen-carrying blood all over their bodies. It means fish can be big and fast: whale sharks can be more than 12 metres long and there are tuna and marlin that can swim at 50 mph!

SURE IS, MATE!

A FISH

A FISH GILL (SHOWING ALL THE FOLDY-UPPY SURFACE AREA)

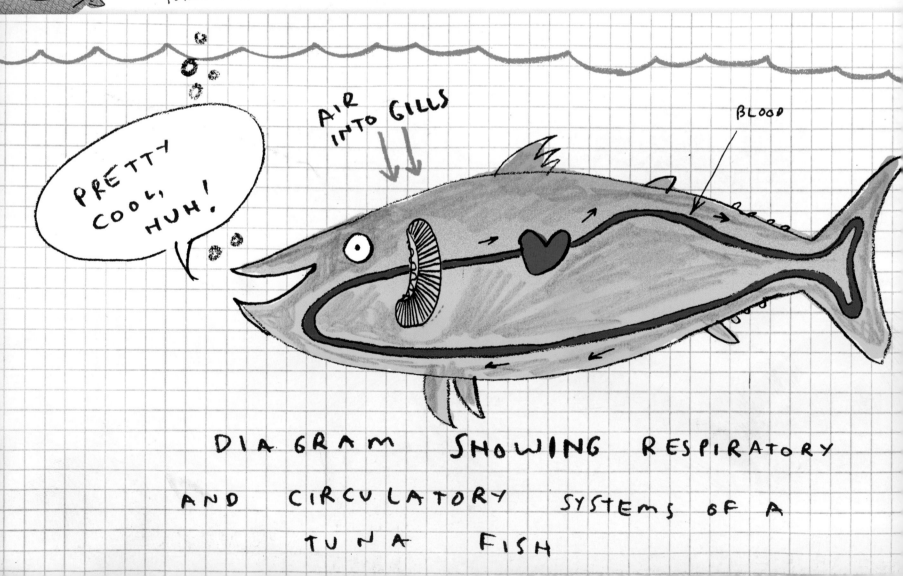

PRETTY COOL, HUH!

AIR INTO GILLS

BLOOD

DIAGRAM SHOWING RESPIRATORY AND CIRCULATORY SYSTEMS OF A TUNA FISH

BOOKS AND TUBES

Gills are fine in water, but they have to stay moist to work and on land they shrivel up in the dry air. So when animals started to live on land they had to evolve in other ways to have lots of moist skin to get their oxygen through.

Spiders have "book lungs", skin folded like the pages of a book, inside air-filled pockets on their tummies. It all works well enough until a spider has to run more than a few tens of metres. Then, book lungs don't work well enough to keep the spider's brain and muscles supplied with oxygen, and the spider just faints. (So two things make giant spiders impossible: snapped legs *and* fainting.)

Insects have a maze of little tubes, called trachea, leading from holes, called spiracles, on the outside of their bodies to deep inside. The deepest tubes are very tiny and lined with thin skin that lets oxygen through to their blood. If the trachea were longer than about a centimetre, not enough air would make it to the bottom of the tubes. With air coming in from spiracles on both sides of their bodies, insects can be twice as thick as the longest trachea — but no thicker. Even the biggest insect in the world, the African goliath beetle, with a body 13 cm long, is little more than a couple of centimetres thick.

GET BIG WITH LUNGS

If spiders and insects had been the only animals around, there might never have been anything bigger on land than a fat beetle. But around 400 million years ago some fish evolved simple lungs that allowed them to swim at the surface and breathe air. This made it possible for the first amphibians to evolve and crawl out onto dry land.

Lungs started out as simple bags, but over millions of years, they got more and more complicated to give a bigger and bigger surface area for getting oxygen. The hearts and blood vessels that worked with them got better too. Mammal lungs are some of the most complicated of all. They are spongy bags, made of millions of tiny air sacs, to give a really HUGE area of thin skin for breathing. (If you spread all the tiny air sacs that make up your lungs out flat, they would cover most of a tennis court!) Mammal hearts are super-efficient. They pump blood fast, delivering oxygen to every cell in a network of minute blood vessels. (If all the little blood vessels from your body were laid end to end, they would reach halfway to the moon.)

Together lungs and new improved sorts of hearts allowed animals on land to evolve into lots of different kinds – reptiles and birds and mammals.

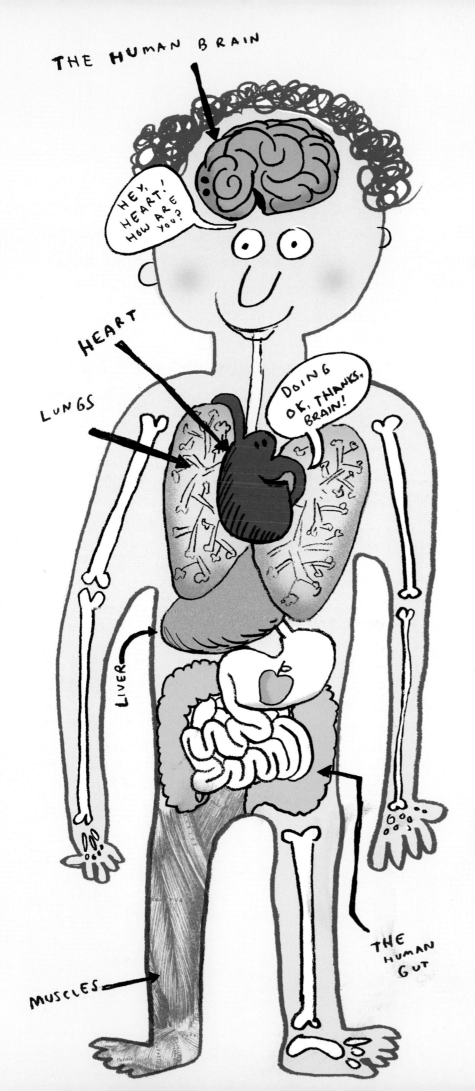

BIG AND COMPLICATED

A simple, single-celled animal just soaks up food and gets rid of waste the same way it gets oxygen — through its skin. But as we've seen, the BTLT rule makes that impossible for bigger animals. So, to do those jobs, bigger animals have internal organs that, just like lungs and gills, pack a huge surface area into a small space.

The lining of the human gut, for example, is folded into millions of tiny fingers that would cover 300 square metres (more than one and a half tennis courts if it was spread out flat). What's more, all those clever, internal organs have to communicate, so they can work together to keep the body healthy…

Thanks to the BTLT rule, the insides of bodies have evolved into very complicated places.

IT'S TOUGH BEING TINY

All in all getting big seems like an awful lot of trouble. Why not stay small and simple like those first animals? Well the answer is that many creatures do just that. Bacteria are very similar to those first little life forms, and they are everywhere (there are ten times more of them living in your body than your body has cells).

The main problem with being so small and simple is that it's very dangerous. All sorts of little accidents like a gust of wind, a shower of rain, an afternoon of hot sun, can wipe out billions of tiny bacteria. They are too small to travel far or fast enough to get out of trouble, and for them, the air seems as thick as soup, and water as sticky as treacle.

There are lots of mouths about that are big enough to swallow tiny bacteria too and, as eyes and brains need many millions of cells to work, they don't have any way of seeing a predator coming or working out what to do about it. It's tough being tiny.

THE NOT-SO-SUPER SUPERHEROES

Bigger, more complicated animals like insects can avoid some of the problems of the super-teeny, super-simple creatures.

They can travel to escape danger and to find food; they have senses to warn them of danger; their brains, though pretty small, can help to solve basic problems; and as we've seen, they can perform like superheroes. But they still suffer a host of perils, just because of their small size.

The BTLT rule that makes them able to lift huge weights and tootle about on the surface of a pond, also means that they have a big surface area for their tiny volume. For animals this small

just getting wet can be fatal. The film of water round a wet, ant-sized body can weigh many times more than the ant does, making it hard for small animals to move when they get soaked. What's more, the surface tension of the water acts like a wrapping of stretchy cellophane, trapping the animal inside so it may even drown!

This is why insects are very wary when they take a drink, and usually do it through long straw-like mouth parts so that there's no risk of any other bit of body getting wet, and drowning them in a raindrop.

COLD-SIZED

A LABRADOR DOG → ← A COMMERSON'S DOLPHIN

Small animals have a bigger outer surface area for their volume than big animals, so they have trouble keeping warm when it's cold; their body heat just leaks out through their skin. This is a real problem for mammals, who can die from cold.

Being small is even more of a problem in water, because water is better than air at taking body heat away — think how freezing you can get in the pool! So one of the smallest mammals that lives all its life in the water is the labrador dog-sized Commerson's dolphin. (Mouse-sized or even rabbit-sized dolphins would cool down too

PART-TIMERS!

fast.) Commerson's dolphins keep warm by eating loads, about 5 kilos of fish and squid every day, and by having very good insulation: a thick layer of fat under the skin.

There are plenty of smaller mammals and birds which visit water to find food — tiny water shrews, small as your finger, and fairy penguins not much larger than a carton of milk, but they couldn't survive the heat-stealing cold full-time.

TINY WATER SHREW

FAIRY PENGUIN

A NOTHER BUSY DAY AHEAD...!

CHOMP!

DIARY OF A COMMERSON'S DOLPHIN

FISH BREAKFAST

MORNING SNACK OF FISH

ELEVENSES (FISH)

FISH LUNCH

followed by FISH TEA BREAK

AFTEROON TEA (WITH FISH)

APERITIFS

DINNER

MIDNIGHT SNACK OF FISH

HOT DINOS

Mammals that live full-time in water are mostly a lot bigger than the Commerson's dolphin because big bodies hold onto their heat better. But being big and warm has other benefits for other sorts of animals too; it may have been the secret of the dinosaurs' success.

Reptiles like snakes, lizards and crocodiles are all cold-blooded. That means they bask in the sun to soak up heat through their skin to get their bodies warm enough to work. But when the sun goes in and it gets cold, the skin that got them warm loses heat just as fast and they cool down — and a cool reptile is a sluggish reptile. The smaller the reptile, the worse it is, because smaller reptiles have bigger skins (surface area) for their volume.

Dinosaurs were reptiles too but the big ones had a much smaller surface area of skin for their volume than smaller modern reptiles. So once they warmed up, they held onto their heat. Many scientists now believe that this allowed bigger dinosaurs to keep warm almost all the time, and if they were warm they could be active.

So it could be the BTLT rule which made T. rex into a fearsome predator!

BIG FOOD

Holding onto their body heat also means that big animals don't need to burn their food fast to keep warm, as smaller animals do; so they can live on quite low quality food. Elephants, the biggest vegetarians, can eat almost anything, dry grass, even bark and wood, but chevrotains — a kind of tiny deer — one of the smallest veggies, are very picky and can only survive by eating the juiciest shoots.

Another reason that bigger animals can survive on rather nasty nosh is that they have the room to digest it. Monkeys are mostly plant-eaters but the toughest bits, like leaves and bark, are very hard to digest and need big complicated guts to do it properly. So only the largest kinds of monkeys, with big round tummies and plenty of room for digestion, can be leaf-eaters. Smaller monkeys don't have room for all that digestive kit and can eat only the juicy bits — like fruits.

BIG MONKEY WITH MORE ROOM FOR DIGESTIVE KIT

SMALL MONKEY WITH LESS DIGESTIVE KIT

AN ELEPHANT

I DON'T KNOW HOW YOU CAN EAT THAT STUFF!

← A CHEVROTAIN

Restaurant des Animals

BIG TRAVELS

Slow food-burning and roomy bodies set big animals up for long distance travel. They can go for longer without food than small animals and there's more room in their big bodies to store food as fat, for when times are lean.

Whales can migrate thousands of miles in the ocean and go for months without eating, whilst most dolphins are homebodies, staying in the same patch of sea.

Wildebeest migrate 1,800 miles a year following the rains and fresh grass across East Africa, whilst the smaller plant eaters have to wait for the rains to come to them.

Big animals are like family cars: they don't use much petrol, they can go for ages without refuelling, and there's lots of room for luggage. Small animals are like sports cars: fast, gas-guzzling and no room for much more than a picnic!

CHEAP FLIGHTS FOR SMALL FLIERS

The world's champion travellers though, aren't big. They're Arctic terns. These little birds, not much bigger than a sparrow, travel an amazing 20,000 miles every year from the Arctic to the Antarctic and back again. That's further than any other creature on the planet.

They can do it because flying, especially for something as light as a tern, is "cheap". It uses very little food for every mile travelled. It's like having a car that will go 5,000 miles on a litre of petrol. Arctic terns stock up on food before they start travelling and put on fat that will fuel them for thousands of miles.

Swimming, walking and running use far more food per mile, so on land and in the water long journeys are only possible for the biggest walkers and swimmers, who need less food for their size than littler animals.

BIGGEST WINNERS

There are advantages to being big that are nothing to do with surface area, or the sort of food an animal can eat. The bigger you are, the fewer predators there are that can make you into their dinner, and the bigger you are, the more fights you can win.

In elephants, the males, or bulls, fight like mad over who mates with the females. The biggest bulls with the biggest tusks are the most successful, which is why male elephants are so much bigger than females.

It's the same for sperm whales, where males can be almost twice as big as the females. In fact, in almost any species where there are fights over females, males are bigger, even if it's just their horns or their tails.

Size differences that don't seem very noticeable to humans, really matter to female animals and birds. Female swallows much prefer to mate with males whose tail feathers are longer ... even if it's only by a few millimetres. And female frogs and toads can tell big males from little ones even in the dark, because the big ones say "ribbet" in a deeper voice.

BIG VOICE – LITTLE VOICE

Bigness isn't always for fighting and showing off, it can be good for communication too. Blue whales keep in touch with each other over huge distances by making deep humming sounds. Only the deepest hums can travel the hundreds of miles to another blue whale, and only very very big animals can make very low-pitched sounds.

Being huge helps blue whales to keep in touch, but being small helps bats find their way in

the dark: they squeak, then listen to the echoes of their voices to get a sound-picture of all that's around them. Low-pitched squeaks would give a very fuzzy sound-picture, so bats use very high-pitched sounds, which give them detailed echo-pictures. And only very teeny little vocal chords can make those high squeaks.

BIG AND SMALL

Being small isn't always a bad thing (just remember the smallest superheroes at the start of the book). Small animals like mice or bats may be snack-sized but, because they are diddy, there are lots of places for them to hide. Small animals don't need much space or food, so there are many ways that they can make a living. A tiger might need a whole forest as its habitat, but a beetle would be happy with a hole in a log.

In fact there can be so many good things about being small that some species that evolved to be big, evolve back into something smaller. Once upon a time gibbons were large, tree-climbing apes, more like chimps. But when they started to get around in the forest by swinging from branch to branch by their arms, having a nice light, little body was very useful. So, over time, they got smaller. Now gibbons are the smallest of all the apes, and can weigh as little as a fat domestic cat.

31

JUST THE RIGHT SIZE

Being the right size is one of the ways that living things can adapt to where they live. "Tiny" is the best bet if where you live is between two grains of sand, but "huge" might be better if your habitat is the whole ocean. So animals and plants come in a mind-boggling range of sizes: the biggest, the blue whale, is 1,000,000,000,000,000,000,000,000 times bigger than the smallest microbe.

But if it wasn't for the BTLT rule, size might almost be the only difference between all these living things. Earth might be populated by creatures that looked like different-sized blobs: little ones living under stones and between grains of sand, medium ones blobbing about on land and huge ones in the sea.

JUST RIGHT

Without the BTLT rule there would be no need for complicated bodies, single-celled blobs of different sizes would do just fine.

To obey the BTLT rule, evolution had to invent living things that weren't just different sizes, but different shapes and patterns too. This has resulted in all sorts of bodies: bodies with one cell or millions, with bones or shells, with gills or lungs, with legs or no legs; bodies that can be "superheroes" and bodies that can think about why they can't be. An ever-changing kaleidoscope of life, a glorious diversity of species, from the very tiniest to the most enormous — and all of them just the right size!

THE SIZE!

INDEX

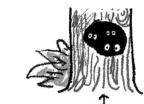
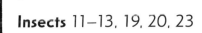

GLOSSARY

Cells tiny units, too small to see, from which all living bodies are made.

Cross section the surface you would see if you sliced through the middle of an object.

Geometry the set of rules that explain the shape and size of objects.

Gills lots of folds of thin skin found either side of a fish's head. They take in oxygen from the water and pass it into the bloodstream.

Gut a long soft tube (also called an "intestine") where food gets digested. Almost all animals have a gut folded up in their belly.

Lungs squishy bags with lots of tiny pockets inside that fill with air when an animal breathes, so that oxygen can pass through the thin skin of the pockets into the blood.

Mammals animals with warm blood and fur who feed their babies on their own milk: mice, elephants, kangaroos, bats and humans are all mammals.

Oxygen a gas that all living creatures need in their bodies to make them work. Animals and insects get it in from the air. Fish get it from water.

Particles very tiny pieces which make up a larger thing. Some things (like water) are made of just one type of particle, but most things (like bodies) are made up of lots of different types of particle.

Surface area how big the outside of something is.

Surface tension a sort of skin that forms on the top of water, where the particles are packed very closely together.

AN ENORMOUS BLUE WHALE

A BIG BEETLE

A BIG GORILLA

WE'RE BIG THINGS

ELEPHANT

ABOUT THE AUTHOR

Nicola Davies is an award-winning author, whose many books for children include *The Promise*, *A First Book of Nature*, *Big Blue Whale*, *Dolphin Baby*, and *The Lion Who Stole My Arm*. She graduated in zoology, studied whales and bats and then worked for the BBC Natural History Unit. Visit Nicola at **www.nicola-davies.com**

"I've been lucky to see dwarf chameleons smaller than my little finger in the wild, and blue whales bigger than my house," she says, "and I couldn't say which was more thrilling."

ABOUT THE ILLUSTRATOR

Neal Layton is an award-winning artist who has illustrated more than sixty books for children, including the other titles in the Animals Science series. He also writes and illustrates his own books, such as *The Story of Everything* and The Mammoth Academy series. Visit Neal at **www.neallayton.co.uk**

About this title, he says, "It's not often you get to draw a giant spider race, but I was grateful to learn they could not actually exist. Phew!"

SOURCES

This is pretty grown up but you can dip in and out of it and you'll learn LOADS:

Animal Kingdom: Life in the Wild – How Wild Animals Survive in their Different Habitats, from Deserts and Jungles to Oceans and the Skies by Michael Chinery (Lorenz Books, 2011)

Biggest smallest, fastest, slowest...they're all in here:

Animal Records by Mark Carwardine (Sterling, 2008)

Car-Sized Crabs and Other Animal Giants by Anna Claybourne (A & C Black, 2013)

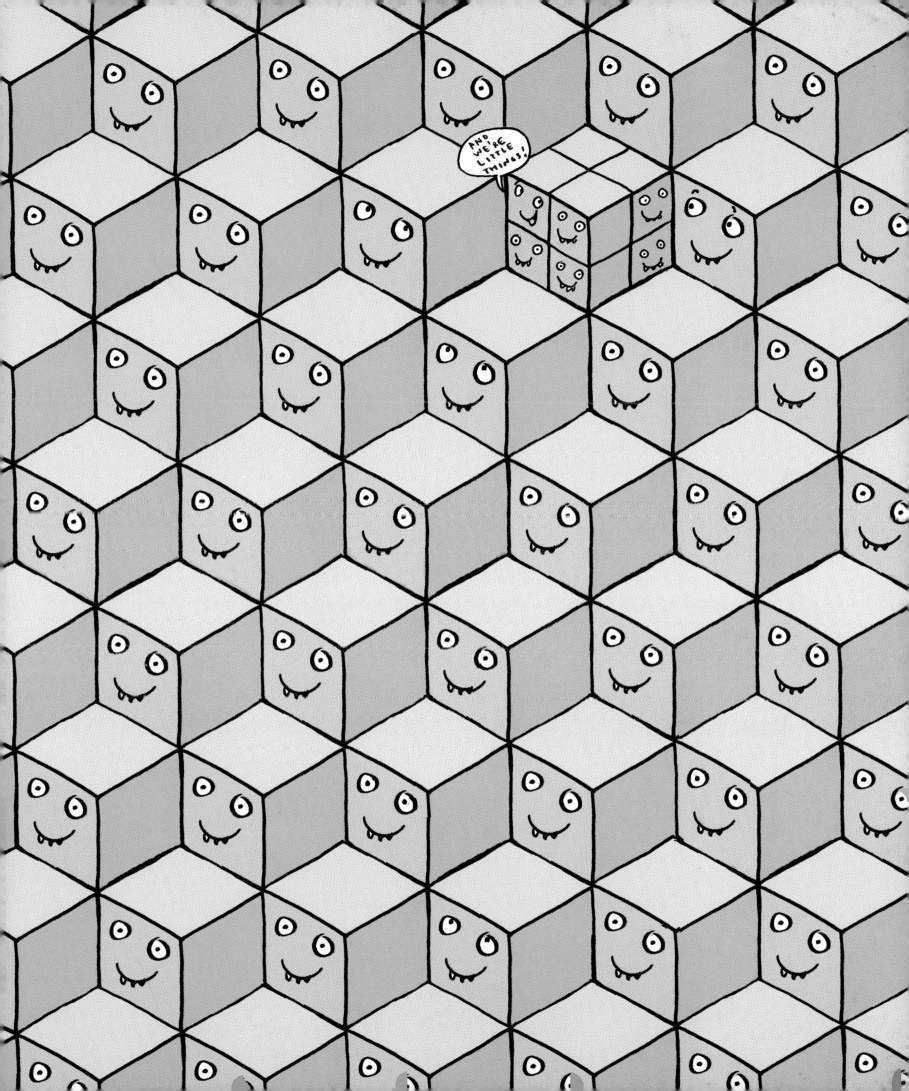

ANIMAL Science

HOW AND WHY ANIMALS DO THE THINGS THEY DO.

ISBN 978-1-4063-5663-2

ISBN 978-1-4063-5665-6

ISBN 978-1-4063-5742-4

ISBN 978-1-4063-5747-9

ISBN 978-1-4063-5748-6

ISBN 978-1-4063-5664-9

If you enjoyed this book, why not collect them all!

Available from all good booksellers

www.walker.co.uk